Philly's Phantom Encounters: Exploring the City's Most Haunted Places

Edward Turner

Published by Oliver Lancaster, 2023.

PHILLY'S PHANTOM ENCOUNTERS: EXPLORING THE CITY'S MOST HAUNTED PLACES

First edition. July 8, 2023.

Copyright © 2023 Edward Turner.

ISBN: 979-8223660156

Written by Edward Turner.

Also by Edward Turner

Ghosts of Paris: Ten Haunted Places in the City of Love

Appalachian Nightmares: The Top 10 Creepy Creatures of the Mountains

Asia's Top Ten Cryptids: Legends, Sightings, and Theories

Evil Women in History: Uncovering the Gruesome Crimes of Ten Notorious Female Killers

Ghosts of London: Ten Haunted Places in The City

Ghosts of New York: Ten Haunted Places in The Big Apple

Missouri Nightmares: The Top 10 Chilling Legends

North America's Top Ten Cryptids: Legends, Sightings, and Theories

Philly's Phantom Encounters: Exploring the City's Most Haunted Places

Philly's Phantom Encounters: Exploring the City's Most Haunted Places

EDWARD TURNER

PHILLY'S PHANTOM ENCOUNTERS: EXPLORING THE CITY'S MOST HAUNTED PLACES

Introduction

What makes Philadelphia a unique and interesting location for ghost hunting enthusiasts?

The history and folklore of the city's haunted places

Why do people seek out spooky experiences?

Chapter 1: Ghosts at the Bellevue

The history and architecture of the Bellevue

Ghost sightings and unexplained phenomena

Chapter 2: Terror at Eastern State Penitentiary

The history and architecture of the prison

Famous inmates and events

Stories of ghost sightings and strange occurrences

Chapter 3: Heidnik's House of Horrors

The crimes committed by Gary Heidnik

His House of Horrors

Ghost sightings and unexplained phenomena

Chapter 4: Elfreth's Alley: Home to Ghosts?

The history and architecture of Elfreth's Alley

Ghost sightings and unexplained phenomena

Chapter 5: USS Olympia: A Haunted Ship?

The history and significance of the naval ship

Ghost sightings and unexplained phenomena

Chapter 6: Spirits at Christ Church Burial Ground

The history and significance of Christ Church Burial Ground

Ghost sightings and unexplained phenomena

Chapter 7: The Powel House: A Haunted Mansion

The history and architecture of the Powel House

Ghost sightings and unexplained phenomena

Chapter 8: The Academy of Music: Home to Ghostly Guests

The history and significance of the Academy of Music

Ghost sightings and unexplained phenomena

Chapter 9: The Philadelphia Zoo: A Jungle of Ghosts?

The history and significance of the zoo

Ghost sightings and unexplained phenomena

PHILLY'S PHANTOM ENCOUNTERS: EXPLORING THE CITY'S MOST HAUNTED PLACES

Chapter 10: The Betsy Ross House: A Revolutionary Spirit

The history and architecture of the Betsy Ross House

Ghost sightings and unexplained phenomena

Reflections on Philly's Phantom Encounters

EDWARD TURNER

Introduction

What makes Philadelphia a unique and interesting location for ghost hunting enthusiasts?

Philadelphia, one of the oldest and most historic cities in the United States, has a rich and intriguing past that has contributed to its reputation as a hub of paranormal activity. From haunted cemeteries to historic mansions, Philadelphia offers a unique and interesting location for ghost hunting enthusiasts.

One of the reasons that Philadelphia is a popular destination for ghost hunting is its rich history. Founded in 1682, Philadelphia was an important city during the American Revolution and was the birthplace of the United States. The city played host to many significant events and figures, including the signing of the Declaration of Independence and the creation of the Liberty Bell, making it a prime location for paranormal activity. The city's numerous historic sites and buildings have witnessed centuries of history and have become the backdrop for countless ghost stories and legends.

Another reason that Philadelphia is a unique location for ghost hunting enthusiasts is its architecture. The city boasts an eclectic mix of architectural styles, from colonial homes to Victorian mansions and Gothic churches. Many of these structures have been around for centuries and have become intertwined with the city's history and folklore, making them prime locations for ghost sightings and other paranormal activity. The Powel House, for example, is a stunning Georgian-style mansion that has been around since the 18th century and is said to be haunted by the ghost of its former owner.

The city's location along the Delaware River also adds to its unique and interesting atmosphere. The river has been an important transportation route for centuries and was once home to bustling ports and docks. Many of these historic sites, such as Penn's Landing and the Independence Seaport Museum, have become popular destinations for ghost hunters due to their connection to the city's maritime history.

Finally, Philadelphia's cultural significance as a hub of art, music, and literature also contributes to its appeal as a destination for paranormal enthusiasts. The city has a rich artistic and literary heritage, with famous writers such as Edgar Allan Poe and Walt Whitman calling Philadelphia home at various points in their lives. The city is also home to numerous museums, galleries, and music venues, some of which are said to be haunted by the ghosts of former patrons and performers.

Philadelphia's rich history, unique architecture, location along the Delaware River, and cultural significance all make it a fascinating destination for ghost hunting enthusiasts. The city's many haunted sites, from historic cemeteries to grand mansions, offer a wealth of opportunities for those seeking to experience paranormal activity and explore the city's eerie and intriguing past.

The history and folklore of the city's haunted places

PHILADELPHIA, THE BIRTHPLACE of America, is a city steeped in rich history and folklore. From the colonial era to the present day, the city has seen its share of triumphs and tragedies, and with that comes stories of ghosts and hauntings that have endured through the centuries. Some of the most famous haunted places in Philadelphia include the Eastern State Penitentiary, the Betsy Ross House, the Powel House, and the Academy of Music, just to name a few.

The Eastern State Penitentiary is perhaps one of the most famous haunted places in the city. This historic prison, which opened in 1829, was designed to be a model of rehabilitation and penance, with a focus on solitary confinement. However, over the years, the prison became overcrowded and conditions deteriorated, leading to reports of abuse, torture, and even death. Many people believe that the spirits of those who suffered and died in the prison still haunt its halls, with reports of ghostly apparitions and unexplained noises.

The Betsy Ross House, where the famous seamstress is said to have sewn the first American flag, is another iconic haunted location in Philadelphia. According to legend, the ghost of Betsy Ross herself still lingers in the house, along with other ghostly apparitions, such as a young girl in a colonial dress and a mysterious man in black.

The Powel House, a historic mansion in the Society Hill neighbourhood, is also said to be haunted by the ghosts of its former occupants. The house was once home to Samuel Powel, who served as the last mayor of Philadelphia under British rule, and his wife, Elizabeth. Visitors and staff have reported seeing the ghostly apparitions of both Samuel and Elizabeth, as well as unexplained sounds and movements throughout the house.

The Academy of Music, one of the oldest opera houses in the country, is another haunted location in Philadelphia. The theatre has a long history of ghostly sightings and unexplained occurrences, such as the sound of footsteps in empty corridors, ghostly apparitions, and strange smells. Some believe that the ghost of a former stagehand named Gus Haenschen still haunts the theatre, as he reportedly died in the building while working on a production.

These stories and many others are part of the rich history and folklore of Philadelphia's haunted places. Whether based on fact or legend, these tales continue to captivate and intrigue people of all ages. They serve as a reminder of the city's past and the people who have lived and died there, as well as the mysteries and unknowns that still linger in the present day. For those interested in exploring the city's haunted places, Philadelphia offers a wealth of opportunities to experience the paranormal and delve into the city's history and folklore.

Why do people seek out spooky experiences?

THE THRILL OF FEAR is a universal experience that has fascinated people for centuries. Whether it's watching a horror movie, visiting a haunted house, or reading ghost stories, there's something about being scared that draws us in. But why do people seek out spooky experiences?

One reason is that fear is a natural human response to danger. Our brains are wired to react to potential threats, triggering the "fight or flight" response. When we experience fear in a controlled environment, such as a horror movie or a haunted house, we get a rush of adrenaline without any real danger. This can be an exhilarating experience that leaves us feeling alive and energised.

In addition to the physical thrill, spooky experiences can also provide a psychological benefit. Fear can be a powerful motivator, pushing us out of our comfort zones and helping us to confront our anxieties. By seeking out scary experiences, we can build resilience and confidence in ourselves. It can also be a way to confront mortality and the unknown, reminding us that we are alive and that life is precious.

Another reason people seek out spooky experiences is for the sense of community it can provide. Ghost tours, haunted attractions, and other spooky events often bring people together who share a common interest in the paranormal. It can be a bonding experience to share scares with others and to explore the unknown together.

Additionally, spooky experiences can offer a break from the mundane and routine of everyday life. They provide an escape from reality and can be a way to inject excitement and novelty into our lives. It's a chance to step outside of our comfort zones and experience something different and thrilling.

Finally, spooky experiences can be a way to connect with history and culture. Many ghost stories and haunted locations have deep roots in local folklore and legends. By seeking out these stories and places, we can learn about the history and culture of a particular area. It can be a way to connect with our past and understand the people and events that shaped our world.

People seek out spooky experiences for a variety of reasons, including the thrill of fear, psychological benefits, sense of community, escape from the mundane, and connection to history and culture. While it may seem counterintuitive to seek out fear, these experiences can be a powerful way to confront our anxieties, build resilience, and connect with the world around us.

PHILLY'S PHANTOM ENCOUNTERS: EXPLORING THE CITY'S MOST HAUNTED PLACES

Chapter 1: Ghosts at the Bellevue

The history and architecture of the Bellevue

The Bellevue is a historic hotel located in the heart of Philadelphia's downtown district. With its grand architecture and elegant furnishings, the Bellevue has been a destination for visitors to the city since it first opened its doors in 1904. But the history of the Bellevue goes back even further, to a time when the area was still a part of the colonial city of Philadelphia.

In the late 18th century, the land on which the Bellevue now stands was part of a larger estate known as the Peters House. The Peters House was one of the largest and most impressive homes in the city, and it was surrounded by gardens and orchards that stretched for miles. But as the city grew, the Peters family was forced to sell off parts of their land to developers, and by the early 20th century, the property had been reduced to just a few acres.

It was during this time that a group of investors led by George Boldt, the former manager of New York's Waldorf-Astoria Hotel, decided to build a new hotel on the site. The hotel would be designed by the famed Philadelphia architect Horace Trumbauer, who had already built several of the city's most iconic buildings, including the Philadelphia Museum of Art and the Free Library of Philadelphia.

Trumbauer's design for the Bellevue was inspired by the great hotels of Europe, with its grand ballrooms, ornate chandeliers, and marble floors. The hotel was also equipped with the latest amenities of the time, including elevators, telephones, and electric lights. When it opened in 1904, the Bellevue was one of the largest and most luxurious hotels in the country, with over 1,000 rooms, 30 shops, and a rooftop garden that offered stunning views of the city.

Over the years, the Bellevue has played host to many famous guests, including Presidents Woodrow Wilson and Franklin D. Roosevelt, as well as numerous celebrities and business leaders. But the hotel has also seen its share of tragedy and hardship. During World War II, the Bellevue was used as a military hospital, and many wounded soldiers were treated there. In the 1970s, the hotel was in danger of being demolished to make way for a new office building, but a group of preservationists managed to save it from destruction.

Today, the Bellevue remains one of the most iconic buildings in Philadelphia, with its grand façade and elegant interiors still attracting visitors from around the world. The hotel has undergone numerous renovations over the years, but its historic architecture and sense of grandeur have remained largely intact. From its ornate ballrooms to its sweeping staircases, the Bellevue is a true masterpiece of design and architecture, and a testament to the city's rich history and culture.

Ghost sightings and unexplained phenomena

THE BELLEVUE HOTEL in Philadelphia is one of the city's most iconic buildings, and it is also home to many ghost sightings. Over the years, the hotel has played host to countless guests, and many of them have reported strange experiences that they believe were caused by spirits.

One of the most famous ghost sightings at the Bellevue is that of a young girl named Caroline. According to legend, Caroline was the daughter of a wealthy family who stayed at the hotel in the early 1900s. One day, she fell down a flight of stairs and died from her injuries. Ever since then, guests at the hotel have reported seeing the ghostly figure of a young girl in a white dress, wandering the hallways.

Another famous ghost sighting at the Bellevue involves a former employee of the hotel named George. According to legend, George was a doorman at the hotel who died on the job. Ever since then, guests have reported seeing his ghostly figure standing in the lobby, wearing his old uniform and holding the door open for them.

In addition to these famous ghost sightings, there have been many other reports of paranormal activity at the Bellevue. Guests have reported hearing strange noises, feeling cold spots, and even seeing apparitions in their rooms.

One particularly eerie story involves a guest who stayed in room 928, which is rumoured to be one of the most haunted rooms in the hotel. According to the guest, she woke up in the middle of the night to find a strange man standing at the foot of her bed, staring at her. When she turned on the light, the man disappeared.

Another famous ghost sighting at the Bellevue involves a woman named Mrs. Brinkley. According to legend, Mrs. Brinkley was a wealthy guest who stayed at the hotel in the 1920s. She was rumoured to have been murdered in her room, and ever since then, guests have reported hearing her ghostly screams in the hallway outside her room.

Despite these ghost sightings, many guests at the Bellevue have reported feeling comforted by the presence of the hotel's spirits. Some believe that the ghosts are simply former guests who loved the hotel so much that they never wanted to leave.

The Bellevue Hotel in Philadelphia has been the site of many unexplained phenomena over the years. From strange noises to inexplicable smells, guests and staff have reported a wide range of mysterious occurrences that seem to defy explanation.

One of the most commonly reported phenomena at the Bellevue is the sound of children laughing and playing in the hallways, even when there are no children staying at the hotel. Many guests have reported hearing the sounds of children's voices and laughter late at night, and some have even reported seeing ghostly apparitions of children running down the hallways.

Another common occurrence at the Bellevue is the smell of perfume or other scents that seem to come out of nowhere. Guests have reported smelling the fragrance of lilacs or roses in the hallways, even when there are no flowers present. Some have even reported smelling cigar smoke, even though smoking is not allowed in the hotel.

In addition to these strange smells and sounds, there have been many reports of objects moving or disappearing without explanation. Guests have reported finding their belongings in different places than where they left them, or discovering that items have gone missing altogether.

Perhaps the most chilling unexplained phenomena at the Bellevue is the feeling of being watched or touched by unseen hands. Many guests have reported feeling a cold breeze or a hand on their shoulder, even when there is no one else around. Some have even reported feeling as though they were being pushed or pulled by an invisible force.

While some may dismiss these experiences as mere coincidences or tricks of the mind, others believe that they are evidence of paranormal activity. The Bellevue has a long and storied history, and many believe that the spirits of former guests and employees still linger within its walls.

Whatever the explanation may be, there is no denying that the Bellevue Hotel is a place of mystery and intrigue. Whether you believe in the paranormal or not, the unexplained phenomena at the Bellevue are a fascinating part of the hotel's history and continue to capture the imaginations of those who visit it.

EDWARD TURNER

Chapter 2: Terror at Eastern State Penitentiary

The history and architecture of the prison

The Eastern State Penitentiary, located in Philadelphia, Pennsylvania, is a historic prison that has played a significant role in the development of the American criminal justice system. The prison was designed to be a place of penance and rehabilitation, rather than simply punishment. It is also known for its unique architecture, which set a new standard for prison design in the 19th century.

The Eastern State Penitentiary was designed by architect John Haviland and opened in 1829. It was considered a revolutionary approach to the design of correctional facilities, as it was the first prison in the United States to implement the system of solitary confinement. The prison was designed to hold up to 250 inmates, who were housed in individual cells that were arranged in a radial pattern around a central hub.

The cells were designed to be self-contained, with each inmate having their own exercise yard, private toilet, and running water. The design of the cells was intended to encourage reflection and repentance, as well as to prevent prisoners from communicating with each other. The prison's founders believed that this system would promote reform and reduce the likelihood of reoffending.

Over the years, the Eastern State Penitentiary became known for its harsh conditions and strict discipline. Prisoners were subjected to long periods of isolation, with many spending years in solitary confinement. The prison also had a strict code of conduct, with prisoners required to maintain complete silence and perform manual labour.

Despite the harsh conditions, the Eastern State Penitentiary was renowned for its architecture. The prison was designed to resemble a castle, with a central tower that rose 85 feet above the prison yard. The walls of the prison were made of grey stone and were 30 feet high and 12 feet thick. The Gothic-style architecture was intended to convey a sense of grandeur and strength, while also serving as a warning to potential wrongdoers.

In addition to the central tower, the prison featured numerous other architectural elements that set it apart from other prisons of the time. The cell blocks were arranged in a radial pattern, with each block radiating out from the central hub like spokes on a wheel. The cells themselves were designed to be octagonal in shape, with vaulted ceilings and small skylights that allowed natural light to enter.

Today, the Eastern State Penitentiary is a National Historic Landmark and a popular tourist attraction. Visitors can tour the prison and learn about its history and architecture, as well as the stories of some of its most famous inmates, including notorious gangster Al Capone.

The Eastern State Penitentiary is a unique and important part of American history. Its innovative approach to prison design and focus on rehabilitation paved the way for modern corrections systems. Its Gothic-style architecture has inspired architects and designers for over a century, and its place in popular culture has made it an iconic symbol of America's criminal justice system.

Famous inmates and events

EASTERN STATE PENITENTIARY, also known as ESP, has been home to some of the most infamous criminals in history. The prison's history spans over 140 years and during that time, it housed some of the most dangerous and notorious criminals in the United States. Here are some of the most famous inmates and events that took place at Eastern State Penitentiary.

Al Capone

PERHAPS THE MOST FAMOUS inmate at Eastern State Penitentiary was Al Capone, the notorious gangster and leader of the Chicago Outfit. Capone was incarcerated at ESP from 1929 to 1930 for carrying a concealed weapon. He was assigned to Cell Block 8, where he lived in relative luxury with a radio, a table lamp, and fine furniture. He was also given permission to decorate his cell with paintings and carpets. Capone's time at Eastern State Penitentiary was marked by his declining health, and he was eventually released on parole due to his poor health.

Slick Willie Sutton

ANOTHER FAMOUS INMATE at Eastern State Penitentiary was Willie Sutton, also known as "Slick Willie." Sutton was a bank robber who gained notoriety for his numerous successful escapes from prison. He was first incarcerated at ESP in 1934 and managed to escape in 1945 by digging a tunnel from his cell to the prison wall. Sutton was later recaptured and returned to Eastern State, where he remained until his transfer to another prison in 1950.

The Escape of Clarence Klinedinst

IN 1943, CLARENCE KLINEDINST, a convicted murderer, managed to escape from Eastern State Penitentiary in one of the most daring prison escapes in history. Klinedinst, along with four other inmates, managed to dig a tunnel under the prison yard and escape through a sewer pipe. Klinedinst remained at large for several weeks before being recaptured.

The Strouds

ROBERT STROUD, ALSO known as the "Birdman of Alcatraz," was originally incarcerated at Eastern State Penitentiary in 1909 for murder. While at ESP, Stroud became interested in bird keeping, and he continued his hobby throughout his incarceration at various other prisons. His mother, Elizabeth Stroud, also served time at Eastern State Penitentiary for prostitution. The Strouds' story was later turned into a popular movie, "Birdman of Alcatraz," which starred Burt Lancaster as Robert Stroud.

Eastern State Penitentiary has a rich history of infamous inmates and events. While the prison is no longer operational, its history and architecture continue to draw tourists and history buffs from all over the world. The prison's eerie and ominous atmosphere is a constant reminder of the dark and turbulent history that took place within its walls.

Stories of ghost sightings and strange occurrences

EASTERN STATE PENITENTIARY in Philadelphia has a long and storied history as one of the most notorious prisons in the United States. It was operational for almost 150 years, and during that time, it housed some of the most dangerous and violent criminals in the country. But with such a dark and bloody history, it should come as no surprise that the prison has a reputation as one of the most haunted places in America.

Over the years, countless visitors and former employees of the prison have reported strange and unexplained occurrences, including ghost sightings, inexplicable noises, and eerie feelings of being watched. These stories have helped to cement Eastern State Penitentiary's reputation as a hotspot for paranormal activity.

One of the most common ghost sightings at Eastern State Penitentiary is that of a figure known as "The Locksmith." The Locksmith is said to be the ghost of a man who was tasked with repairing the prison's cell doors. According to legend, he was murdered by inmates who were desperate to escape, and his ghost has been haunting the prison ever since. Visitors to the prison have reported seeing The Locksmith's ghostly figure, often accompanied by the sound of keys jingling in the distance.

Another famous ghost sighting at Eastern State Penitentiary is that of Al Capone, the notorious gangster who was incarcerated at the prison in the 1920s. Capone was famously imprisoned in a luxurious cell with amenities like a radio, a table lamp, and even a set of oriental rugs. But despite his plush accommodations, Capone is said to have been haunted by the ghost of James Clark, one of the victims of the St. Valentine's Day Massacre. According to legend, Capone's cell was plagued by strange noises and eerie apparitions, including the ghost of Clark, who would appear to him at night.

In addition to these famous ghost sightings, there have been countless reports of unexplained phenomena at Eastern State Penitentiary. Visitors to the prison have reported feeling cold spots and sudden drops in temperature, even on warm days. Others have reported hearing unexplained noises, like footsteps and whispered voices, echoing through the empty cell blocks. And some visitors have even reported feeling a sense of being touched or pushed by an unseen presence.

One of the most notorious areas of the prison for unexplained phenomena is Cellblock 12, also known as the "Hospital Block." This section of the prison was where sick and mentally ill inmates were kept, and it is said to be haunted by the ghosts of these tormented souls. Visitors to Cellblock 12 have reported hearing cries and moans coming from empty cells, and some have even reported seeing ghostly figures moving through the hallways.

Whether or not you believe in ghosts and the paranormal, there's no denying that Eastern State Penitentiary is a fascinating and eerie place. With its long and bloody history, it's no wonder that the prison has become a magnet for ghost hunters and paranormal enthusiasts from around the world. And with so many unexplained phenomena and ghostly sightings, it's easy to see why Eastern State Penitentiary is considered one of the most haunted places in America.

Eastern State Penitentiary is known not only for its infamous past, but also for the numerous strange occurrences that have been reported over the years. The prison has long been rumoured to be haunted, with many visitors and employees claiming to have witnessed unexplainable phenomena.

Here are some of the strange occurrences that have been reported at Eastern State Penitentiary:

Shadowy Figures

MANY VISITORS HAVE reported seeing shadowy figures moving through the cell blocks, even though there is no one there. Some have reported seeing these figures vanish into thin air, or disappear into the walls.

Mysterious Sounds

EMPLOYEES AND VISITORS have reported hearing strange sounds coming from the empty cell blocks, including footsteps, voices, and screams. Some have even reported hearing the sounds of old-fashioned music, as if from a radio or gramophone.

Moving Objects

SEVERAL PEOPLE HAVE reported seeing objects move on their own, including doors and cell doors opening and closing by themselves. Some have even reported seeing objects levitate or fly through the air.

Cold Spots

MANY VISITORS AND EMPLOYEES have reported feeling sudden drops in temperature in certain areas of the prison. Some have reported feeling a sudden chill in the air, or feeling as if they were standing in a cold spot.

Apparitions

SEVERAL VISITORS AND employees have reported seeing ghostly apparitions throughout the prison. These apparitions often appear as misty figures or dark shadows, and are said to vanish as quickly as they appear.

Strange Smells

SOME VISITORS AND EMPLOYEES have reported smelling strange odours throughout the prison, including the scent of tobacco smoke, perfume, and even the smell of cooking food.

Electrical Disturbances

MANY PEOPLE HAVE REPORTED experiencing electrical disturbances while visiting the prison. This includes lights flickering on and off, and electronic devices malfunctioning.

Unexplained Feelings

SOME VISITORS AND EMPLOYEES have reported feeling uneasy or uncomfortable in certain areas of the prison, even though there is no apparent reason for it. Some have even reported feeling as if they were being watched or followed.

These strange occurrences have been reported by numerous visitors and employees of Eastern State Penitentiary over the years. While some people dismiss them as mere coincidence or imagination, others believe that they are evidence of the prison's haunted past. Whatever the explanation may be, there is no denying that Eastern State Penitentiary is a place that continues to captivate and intrigue visitors from all over the world.

EDWARD TURNER

Chapter 3: Heidnik's House of Horrors

The crimes committed by Gary Heidnik

Gary Michael Heidnik was an American serial killer and rapist who was convicted of the kidnapping, rape, torture, and murder of six women between 1986 and 1987. Heidnik was born on November 22, 1943, in Cleveland, Ohio. He was raised in a troubled family and had a difficult childhood. He was diagnosed with a mild form of schizophrenia in the 1960s and was committed to several psychiatric institutions throughout his life.

In the 1970s, Heidnik started a successful business, the United Church of the Ministers of God, and used his wealth to buy properties in Philadelphia, Pennsylvania. He was known to be a loner and had few friends. He was also a collector of firearms and had a fascination with torture and sexual domination.

In November 1986, Heidnik abducted his first victim, Josefina Rivera, from a bus stop in Philadelphia. He took her to his home at 3520 North Marshall Street, where he held her captive in a hole in the basement. Heidnik's house was later dubbed "the House of Horrors" by the media.

Over the next few months, Heidnik kidnapped five more women and held them captive in his basement. He raped and tortured them and kept them in chains. He also used electric shocks, starvation, and beatings to control them. Heidnik forced his captives to perform sexual acts with each other and with him. He even impregnated two of them.

In March 1987, one of the women, Jacqueline Askins, managed to escape and told the police about the other captives. When the police arrived at Heidnik's house, they found the five remaining women chained in the basement. Two of them were dead, and the others were severely malnourished and injured.

Heidnik was arrested and charged with six counts of murder, kidnapping, rape, and torture. He was found guilty and sentenced to death in July 1988. Heidnik was executed by lethal injection on July 6, 1999.

The crimes committed by Gary Heidnik were some of the most gruesome and shocking in American history. He was known to be a sadistic and depraved individual who enjoyed inflicting pain on his victims. The House of Horrors where he committed his crimes has become a symbol of terror and horror.

Heidnik's case also brought attention to the issue of mental illness and its treatment in the United States. Heidnik was diagnosed with schizophrenia, but his condition was not properly treated, and he was able to commit his crimes without being detected. His case highlighted the need for better mental health care and the importance of identifying and treating mental illness.

The legacy of Gary Heidnik lives on, not only in the memories of his victims and their families but also in the public consciousness. Heidnik's crimes were a reminder of the evil that can exist in the world and the need for vigilance and action to prevent such atrocities from occurring again.

His House of Horrors

GARY HEIDNIK'S HOUSE is known as the House of Horrors due to the gruesome and terrifying crimes that were committed within its walls. Located at 3520 North Marshall Street in the Nicetown-Tioga neighbourhood of Philadelphia, the house still stands as a dark reminder of Heidnik's atrocities.

The house is a three-story brick row house with a small front yard and a narrow driveway. It is a typical Philadelphia row house, similar to the ones that can be found throughout the city. From the outside, it appears unremarkable and nondescript, blending in with the other houses on the street.

However, the interior of the house tells a different story. When police officers first entered the house on March 24, 1987, they were confronted with a scene of unimaginable horror. The house was filled with an overpowering stench, and the floors were covered in filth, rotting food, and human waste. The walls were adorned with Nazi and Satanic symbols, and the basement contained a pit that had been dug out of the floor.

The basement was where Heidnik had kept his captives. He had constructed a makeshift dungeon with cinder block walls and a dirt floor. The pit was four feet deep and six feet long, with a drain at the bottom. Heidnik had installed an electric shock device in the ceiling, which he used to torture his captives. The walls were covered in bloodstains, and there were chains and handcuffs hanging from the ceiling.

The rest of the house was no less horrifying. The second floor contained a bedroom where Heidnik had kept one of his captives, Josefina Rivera. She had been shackled to a bed for weeks and had been repeatedly raped and tortured by Heidnik. The third floor contained another bedroom, which Heidnik had used as his own living quarters. It was filled with Nazi memorabilia and other disturbing items.

The house was a scene of unspeakable horror, and it is difficult to imagine the terror that Heidnik's victims must have felt. The house has been abandoned since Heidnik's arrest in 1987, and it has become a macabre attraction for ghost hunters and curiosity-seekers. The house has been vandalised and stripped of anything valuable, but the ghosts of Heidnik's victims are said to still haunt the house, unable to find peace after their brutal deaths.

The House of Horrors is a chilling reminder of the depravity that humans are capable of. It is a place of unspeakable horror, where innocent lives were destroyed by a madman. The house still stands as a testament to the evil that can lurk within the human heart, and it is a warning to all of us to be vigilant against the darkness that can threaten to consume us.

Ghost sightings and unexplained phenomena

THE HOUSE WHERE GARY Heidnik committed his heinous crimes has a dark history and a reputation for being one of the most haunted places in Philadelphia. Even after the house was demolished in 1999, reports of ghostly sightings and strange phenomena persist to this day.

Many who lived near the house reported eerie feelings and strange occurrences. Some claimed to hear voices and screams coming from the property, even though it was vacant. Others said they saw strange lights or shadows moving around the property.

Visitors to the site of the former house have reported feeling uneasy or experiencing unusual sensations. Some say they felt like they were being watched or followed by an unseen presence. Others report seeing ghostly apparitions, including figures that resemble Gary Heidnik himself.

One of the most frequently reported sightings at the site is the ghost of Heidnik's last victim, Josefina Rivera. Rivera was one of six women who Heidnik kidnapped and held captive in the basement of the house. She managed to escape and led police to the property, ultimately leading to Heidnik's arrest. Some claim to have seen her ghost wandering the site of the former house, searching for her lost companions.

Another commonly reported sighting is the ghost of Gary Heidnik himself. Witnesses have reported seeing a figure that matches Heidnik's appearance, often accompanied by a feeling of extreme cold or an unpleasant odour. Some claim to have heard Heidnik's voice, whispering or speaking incoherently.

There have also been reports of other ghostly apparitions at the site, including figures that resemble the other victims of Heidnik's crimes. Some claim to have seen strange lights or heard unexplained noises, such as footsteps or doors opening and closing.

Despite the demolition of the house and the passing of many years since the crimes were committed, the site where Gary Heidnik committed his gruesome crimes remains a place of unease and discomfort for many. The stories of ghostly sightings and strange occurrences serve as a reminder of the dark history of this once-quiet neighbourhood, and the atrocities committed by one of America's most notorious serial killers.

The house where Gary Heidnik committed his heinous crimes is known as the "House of Horrors" due to the gruesome nature of the acts that took place inside. It is also said to be a place of unexplained phenomena and strange occurrences.

Many who have visited the house, which is located at 3520 North Marshall Street in Philadelphia, have reported feeling uneasy and sensing a dark presence inside. Some have reported hearing strange noises, such as footsteps or the sound of chains dragging along the floor, despite there being no one else in the house. Others have reported feeling sudden drops in temperature or being touched by an unseen force.

There have also been reports of apparitions and shadow figures seen inside the house. Some claim to have seen the ghostly figure of Gary Heidnik himself, while others have reported seeing the spirits of his victims or other unidentified ghosts. In fact, the house has been the subject of paranormal investigations and featured on TV shows such as "Ghost Adventures" and "Paranormal Lockdown."

One particularly eerie occurrence happened during an investigation by the "Ghost Adventures" team. While they were exploring the basement, they heard a strange growling noise and captured it on their audio recorder. Upon playback, the noise was found to be a guttural growl that could not be explained by any natural means.

Despite the house being sold and renovated multiple times since the crimes were committed, the reports of unexplained phenomena and ghostly sightings have persisted. Some speculate that the dark energy left behind by Heidnik's crimes has tainted the house and attracted malevolent spirits. Others believe that the spirits of the victims are trapped inside, unable to move on due to the traumatic nature of their deaths.

Regardless of the reason, it is clear that the house where Gary Heidnik committed his crimes remains a place of intense energy and unexplained phenomena. Visitors are warned to approach with caution and respect, as the spirits that linger inside may not be friendly.

EDWARD TURNER

Chapter 4: Elfreth's Alley: Home to Ghosts?

The history and architecture of Elfreth's Alley

Elfreth's Alley is a historic street located in the Old City neighbourhood of Philadelphia. It is the oldest continuously occupied residential street in the United States, and it is home to thirty-two historic homes and buildings that date back to the early 1700s.

The street is named after Jeremiah Elfreth, a blacksmith and property owner who purchased the land in 1702. Elfreth subdivided the land and sold it to other property owners, and by the mid-1700s, the street was home to a diverse group of artisans, tradespeople, and merchants.

The homes on Elfreth's Alley were built in a variety of architectural styles, reflecting the changing tastes and trends of the time. Many of the homes were built in the Georgian style, with red brick facades, white trim, and symmetrical designs. Some of the homes also feature Federal and Victorian elements, such as ornate wrought iron balconies and decorative cornices.

One of the most notable features of Elfreth's Alley is the cobblestone pavement, which was originally laid in the 18th century. The stones were originally brought from England as ballast in ships, and they were later used to pave the streets of Philadelphia. Today, the cobblestones are a popular feature of the street, and they give visitors a sense of what the neighbourhood would have looked and felt like in the past.

Over the years, Elfreth's Alley has undergone many changes and renovations, but the street has managed to maintain its historic charm and character. Today, the homes on the street are owned and maintained by the Elfreth's Alley Association, a nonprofit organisation dedicated to preserving the historic integrity of the street and educating the public about its rich history.

Visitors to Elfreth's Alley can take a self-guided tour of the homes and learn about the lives of the people who lived there. The homes are decorated with period furniture and artefacts, giving visitors a glimpse into what life was like in colonial Philadelphia. The street is also home to a number of shops, galleries, and restaurants, which offer visitors a chance to experience the vibrant culture and community of the Old City neighbourhood.

Overall, Elfreth's Alley is a unique and fascinating piece of American history. Its beautiful homes, cobblestone streets, and rich cultural heritage make it a must-see destination for anyone interested in the history and architecture of Philadelphia.

Ghost sightings and unexplained phenomena

ELFRETH'S ALLEY IS not only one of the oldest continuously inhabited residential streets in America but also one of the most haunted. It's said that the houses along the alley are home to ghosts that still linger from the past.

One of the most famous ghost stories on Elfreth's Alley is that of the ghostly woman who is said to haunt one of the houses. The story goes that a woman who lived in one of the houses on the alley died under mysterious circumstances. Her ghostly apparition has been seen by many residents and visitors, standing in the windows of the house, or walking up and down the alley. Some have reported hearing her cries and moans echoing through the narrow street late at night.

Another story is about the ghost of a little girl who roams around one of the houses on the alley. She's often seen playing with a ball, and some say she's the spirit of a child who died in one of the houses. The sound of her laughter and the sight of the ball bouncing down the street can often be heard and seen late at night.

Another ghostly tale is that of the shadowy figure that's often seen in the alley. It's said that this shadowy figure is the ghost of a man who died in one of the houses. He's often seen lurking in the shadows, watching the living as they go about their business on the alley. Some have reported feeling an intense feeling of dread and fear when they see him.

There are also stories of a ghostly cat that roams the alley. It's said that this cat belonged to one of the residents who lived on the alley, and when the cat died, its spirit remained behind. Some have reported seeing the cat's ghostly form late at night, and others have felt its presence but never seen it.

One of the most haunted houses on the alley is said to be the Betsy Ross House, where the famous seamstress and flag maker once lived. Visitors and staff members have reported strange occurrences such as doors opening and closing on their own, footsteps heard in empty rooms, and the sensation of being watched by an unseen presence.

Many believe that the ghosts of Elfreth's Alley are the spirits of the early residents who lived there. These ghostly apparitions are said to be the remnants of the people who once called the alley home, and their spirits still linger, unable to leave the place they loved so much.

Despite the ghostly tales that surround Elfreth's Alley, many visitors still flock to the street to catch a glimpse of the historic homes and soak up the rich history and atmosphere of the area. Whether or not you believe in the paranormal, the stories of the ghosts of Elfreth's Alley are a testament to the enduring power of history and the human spirit.

Elfreth's Alley is one of the oldest residential streets in the United States, and as such, it is steeped in history and tradition. While many of the houses on the alley have been restored and preserved over the years, some still retain their original features and furnishings, giving visitors a unique glimpse into the past. However, along with this rich history comes tales of unexplained phenomena that have occurred in the houses along the alley.

One of the most common unexplained occurrences reported on Elfreth's Alley is the sound of footsteps. Many visitors have reported hearing the sound of footsteps on the stairs or in empty rooms, even when no one else is around. Some have even reported the feeling of being touched or pushed, as if someone or something is trying to get their attention.

Another common occurrence is the presence of cold spots or sudden drops in temperature. Many visitors have reported feeling a sudden chill or drop in temperature as they walk through the houses on the alley, even in rooms that are supposed to be warm and well-heated. Some have even reported seeing their breath in front of them, as if they were standing outside in the cold.

Other unexplained phenomena reported on Elfreth's Alley include strange odours, the sound of voices or whispers, and the feeling of being watched. Some visitors have even reported seeing apparitions or shadows moving through the rooms, or experiencing a feeling of intense dread or fear for no apparent reason.

One particularly eerie incident occurred in one of the houses on Elfreth's Alley, where a young girl was said to have been murdered by her father in the 1800s. Visitors to the house have reported seeing the ghostly apparition of the young girl, as well as hearing her voice or feeling her presence. Some have even reported the feeling of being touched or brushed past by the ghostly figure, as if she were trying to communicate with them.

Despite the numerous reports of unexplained phenomena on Elfreth's Alley, sceptics remain unconvinced. Some argue that the old houses are simply creaky and draughty, and that the sounds and sensations reported by visitors are nothing more than the natural quirks of an old building. Others point to the power of suggestion, noting that people who visit the alley are often primed to expect something spooky or unusual, which can influence their perceptions and interpretations of what they experience.

Regardless of the explanations, the stories of unexplained phenomena on Elfreth's Alley continue to fascinate and intrigue visitors from around the world. Whether you believe in ghosts and spirits or not, a visit to this historic alley is sure to be an unforgettable experience.

PHILLY'S PHANTOM ENCOUNTERS: EXPLORING THE CITY'S MOST HAUNTED PLACES

Chapter 5: USS Olympia: A Haunted Ship?

The history and significance of the naval ship

The USS Olympia is a naval ship with a rich history and significant historical significance. It was commissioned in 1895 and was the flagship of the US Navy in the Spanish-American War. The ship was a key part of the US fleet that engaged in the Battle of Manila Bay, where it played a significant role in the defeat of the Spanish fleet. The USS Olympia also played a role in the Philippine-American War and World War I.

The USS Olympia was built by the Union Iron Works in San Francisco, California. It was designed as a protected cruiser, with a speed of up to 21 knots and armed with 8-inch guns. The ship was named after the city of Olympia, Washington, and was launched in 1892.

The USS Olympia was commissioned on November 5, 1895, and served as the flagship of the US Navy's Asiatic Squadron under Admiral George Dewey. The ship played a significant role in the Battle of Manila Bay, which took place on May 1, 1898, during the Spanish-American War. The battle saw the US Navy defeat the Spanish fleet in the Philippines, and the USS Olympia played a key role in the victory.

After the Spanish-American War, the USS Olympia was used to patrol the Philippines and take part in the Philippine-American War. The ship was decommissioned in 1906 but was recommissioned in 1916 for service in World War I. During the war, the USS Olympia was used for training and patrol duties in the Atlantic.

The USS Olympia was decommissioned for the final time in 1922 and was preserved as a museum ship. The ship was moved to Philadelphia in 1957 and has been part of the Independence Seaport Museum since 1996. The USS Olympia is a National Historic Landmark and is the oldest steel warship afloat in the world.

The USS Olympia is a significant historical artefact that provides a glimpse into the history of the US Navy and the country's military past. The ship played a significant role in the Spanish-American War and was part of a pivotal moment in US history when the country emerged as a world power. The ship's design and construction also represent a significant technological achievement, as it was one of the first steel warships built by the US Navy.

In addition to its historical significance, the USS Olympia is also an impressive example of naval architecture. The ship's design reflects the evolution of naval technology and engineering during the late 19th century, with its advanced propulsion system, protective armour, and powerful armament. The ship also features an elegant, streamlined design that reflects the aesthetic preferences of the era.

The USS Olympia is a significant symbol of American naval power and technological innovation. It is an important historical artefact that provides insight into the country's past and the evolution of naval technology. The ship's preservation as a museum ship ensures that its legacy will continue to be celebrated and studied by future generations.

Ghost sightings and unexplained phenomena

THE USS OLYMPIA HAS a storied history as a naval ship, having served in the Spanish-American War and World War I. However, along with its rich history and impressive achievements, the ship also has a reputation for being haunted.

Over the years, many visitors to the ship have reported strange occurrences and ghostly sightings. Some have claimed to see the ghost of a sailor standing at attention on the deck, while others have reported hearing unexplained footsteps and voices. Some have even claimed to feel a presence following them around the ship.

One of the most famous ghost stories associated with the USS Olympia is that of the sailor who is said to have died on board during World War I. According to the legend, the sailor was struck by a shell and died instantly. His body was then placed in the ship's sick bay, where it remained for several days until it could be properly disposed of.

Today, many visitors to the ship claim to feel a presence in the sick bay and report strange occurrences in the area. Some have even reported seeing the ghostly figure of a sailor lying on one of the beds.

Another famous ghost story associated with the USS Olympia involves the ship's engine room. According to some accounts, a sailor was killed in the engine room during World War I when he was trapped by one of the ship's engines. Since then, many visitors to the engine room have reported hearing strange noises and feeling a presence in the area.

Other visitors have reported seeing ghostly figures in the ship's passageways and hearing strange whispers in the dark. Some have even reported feeling cold spots and sudden drops in temperature.

Despite the numerous reports of ghostly activity on the USS Olympia, there are those who remain sceptical. Some argue that the stories are simply urban legends, while others suggest that they may be the result of overactive imaginations or the power of suggestion.

Regardless of whether the stories are true or not, there is no denying the eerie atmosphere that pervades the ship. For many visitors, the USS Olympia is not just a historic naval vessel, but also a site of paranormal activity and ghostly encounters.

The USS Olympia has a storied history, having served as a naval vessel in the Spanish-American War and World War I. However, along with its impressive legacy, the ship has also been the site of many mysterious and unexplained occurrences that have baffled crew members and visitors alike.

PHILLY'S PHANTOM ENCOUNTERS: EXPLORING THE CITY'S MOST HAUNTED PLACES

One of the most common paranormal experiences reported on the USS Olympia is the sensation of being watched or followed. Many people have reported feeling as if they are being followed or that they are not alone on the ship, even when no one else is around. Others have reported feeling as if someone is breathing down their neck, or have heard footsteps following them through the corridors.

Another eerie phenomenon that has been reported on the USS Olympia is the presence of phantom smells. Many people have reported smelling unusual scents, such as cigar smoke or the scent of a woman's perfume, even though no one else is around. Others have reported the smell of burning wood or the scent of sea water, despite the fact that the ship has been docked in Philadelphia for many years.

In addition to these experiences, many visitors to the USS Olympia have reported hearing unexplained sounds and voices. Some have reported hearing the sounds of footsteps or doors opening and closing, even when no one else is on the ship. Others have reported hearing whispers or even full conversations, though they are unable to determine where the sounds are coming from.

Perhaps the most chilling paranormal experience reported on the USS Olympia is the presence of ghostly apparitions. Many people have reported seeing the ghostly figure of a man in a sailor's uniform, believed to be the spirit of a former crew member who died on the ship. Others have reported seeing the ghostly figure of a woman in a white dress, believed to be the spirit of a woman who drowned while on board the ship.

One particularly eerie experience occurred in the ship's engine room, where crew members have reported feeling as if someone is watching them. Some have even reported feeling as if they are being touched or pushed by an unseen force, leading many to believe that the engine room is particularly haunted.

Despite the many reports of paranormal activity on the USS Olympia, there is no clear explanation for why these phenomena occur. Some believe that the ship is haunted by the spirits of former crew members who died on board, while others believe that the ship's history and the traumatic events that occurred during its service have left an imprint on the ship's environment.

Whatever the explanation may be, the USS Olympia remains a popular destination for paranormal enthusiasts and those seeking to experience the ship's eerie atmosphere. While some may remain sceptical of the ship's paranormal reputation, those who have experienced its unexplained phenomena firsthand have no doubt that there is something strange and otherworldly about the historic naval vessel.

PHILLY'S PHANTOM ENCOUNTERS: EXPLORING THE CITY'S MOST HAUNTED PLACES

Chapter 6: Spirits at Christ Church Burial Ground

The history and significance of Christ Church Burial Ground

Christ Church Burial Ground is located in Philadelphia, Pennsylvania, and is the final resting place of some of America's most famous Founding Fathers, including Benjamin Franklin, his wife Deborah, and four other signers of the Declaration of Independence. The cemetery was founded in 1719 and is part of the historic Christ Church complex, which is still an active Episcopal parish.

The cemetery was established as a response to the city's rapidly growing population and the overcrowding of existing church cemeteries. In 1732, Christ Church purchased the land for the burial ground, which was located on the outskirts of the city at the time. The cemetery quickly became popular among Philadelphia's elite, who were buried in elaborate tombs and monuments.

Over the years, the cemetery has undergone several renovations and expansions. In the late 19th century, a wall was built around the cemetery to provide more security and privacy for the graves. The cemetery was also redesigned to make it more park-like, with winding paths and landscaped gardens.

In addition to the graves of the Founding Fathers, the cemetery contains the remains of many other notable figures, including several Revolutionary War heroes, early American statesmen, and prominent Philadelphia citizens. The cemetery is also home to several unique and historic grave markers, including a number of iron grave covers that were popular in the early 18th century.

Today, Christ Church Burial Ground is a popular tourist destination and a significant part of Philadelphia's cultural heritage. The cemetery is open to visitors year-round and offers guided tours that highlight the lives and legacies of the famous figures buried there.

In addition to its historical significance, the cemetery is also notable for its architecture and art. The tombs and monuments in the cemetery are excellent examples of 18th and 19th-century American funerary art and reflect the changing styles and tastes of the time. Some of the most impressive monuments in the cemetery include the Franklin family tomb, which features a large marble slab inscribed with Benjamin Franklin's name, and the memorial to Dr. Benjamin Rush, a signer of the Declaration of Independence and a prominent physician and educator.

The cemetery also contains several beautiful and historic buildings, including the Christ Church Rectory, which dates back to 1755 and is one of the oldest buildings in the city. The rectory is a prime example of Georgian architecture and has been beautifully restored and preserved over the years.

Overall, Christ Church Burial Ground is a significant part of American history and a testament to the lives and legacies of the Founding Fathers and other important figures who helped shape the nation. Its historic architecture and art, combined with its beautiful and peaceful setting, make it a must-see destination for anyone visiting Philadelphia.

Ghost sightings and unexplained phenomena

CHRIST CHURCH BURIAL Ground, located in the Old City neighbourhood of Philadelphia, is the final resting place of some of America's most prominent founding fathers, including Benjamin Franklin, Robert Morris, and Benjamin Rush. As one of the oldest cemeteries in the United States, it has a rich history, dating back to the early 18th century.

Over the years, many visitors to the cemetery have reported eerie experiences and ghost sightings, adding to the site's mysterious allure. Here are some of the most notable stories of ghost sightings at Christ Church Burial Ground:

Benjamin Franklin's Ghost

VISITORS TO THE CEMETERY have reported seeing the ghost of Benjamin Franklin wandering among the graves. Some have claimed to see him near his own grave, while others have seen him near the graves of his family members. His ghost is said to appear as a misty figure dressed in colonial-era clothing.

The Two Sisters

ONE OF THE MOST FAMOUS ghost stories associated with the cemetery involves two sisters who were buried there in the early 19th century. According to the legend, the sisters were buried side by side, but their graves were later moved to different locations. Visitors have reported seeing the ghosts of two young women dressed in 19th-century clothing walking hand in hand through the cemetery.

The Unmarked Grave

ONE OF THE MOST MYSTERIOUS aspects of the cemetery is an unmarked grave located near Benjamin Franklin's grave. No one knows for sure who is buried there, but some believe it may be Franklin's son William, who was a loyalist during the Revolutionary War. Visitors to the cemetery have reported feeling a sense of unease or sadness when standing near the unmarked grave.

The Moving Tombstones

SOME VISITORS HAVE reported seeing tombstones move or change position on their own. One of the most famous examples of this occurred in the early 20th century, when a tombstone was found in the middle of an alley that had previously been clear.

The Shadowy Figure

VISITORS HAVE REPORTED seeing a shadowy figure moving among the graves at night. Some have described the figure as a man in a long coat, while others have said it appears as a misty or ghostly presence.

Despite these stories, there are no official records of any paranormal activity at Christ Church Burial Ground. However, the site's long and storied history, coupled with the presence of some of America's most famous figures, continues to attract visitors seeking a glimpse of the past and perhaps a ghostly encounter.

Christ Church Burial Ground is a historic cemetery located in Philadelphia, Pennsylvania. It was established in 1719, and it is the final resting place of several notable figures, including Benjamin Franklin, his wife, Deborah, and several signers of the Declaration of Independence. The cemetery is well known for its historical significance, but it is also infamous for its reported paranormal activity.

One of the most common reported phenomena at the cemetery is the sighting of ghostly apparitions. Visitors have reported seeing figures moving among the headstones, and some have even claimed to have seen the ghostly figure of Benjamin Franklin himself. Others have reported seeing apparitions of soldiers from the Revolutionary War or Civil War, as well as figures in 18th-century clothing.

Another common phenomenon reported at the cemetery is unexplained noises. Visitors have reported hearing footsteps and whispers, even when there is no one else around. Some have even claimed to hear the sound of a church bell ringing, even though there is no church nearby. Others have reported hearing the sound of laughter or voices, as if there were a gathering of people nearby.

There have also been reports of objects moving on their own. Some visitors have reported seeing headstones or other objects shift or move, even when there is no one around. Others have reported feeling a cold breeze or sudden drop in temperature, which is often associated with paranormal activity.

Perhaps one of the most eerie phenomena reported at Christ Church Burial Ground is the feeling of being watched or followed. Visitors have reported feeling as if someone or something is following them as they move through the cemetery, and some have even reported feeling as if they were being touched or pushed.

It is worth noting that many of these reported phenomena can be attributed to natural causes, such as wind or animals moving through the area. However, some visitors remain convinced that there is something supernatural at work in the cemetery.

Despite the reported paranormal activity, the cemetery remains a popular destination for tourists and history buffs. In addition to the notable figures buried there, the cemetery also features several historic monuments and markers, which provide a fascinating glimpse into Philadelphia's rich history.

PHILLY'S PHANTOM ENCOUNTERS: EXPLORING THE CITY'S MOST HAUNTED PLACES

Chapter 7: The Powel House: A Haunted Mansion

The history and architecture of the Powel House

The Powel House, located in Philadelphia, Pennsylvania, is a historic landmark that was built in the mid-18th century. The house was constructed by Samuel Powel, a wealthy merchant and politician, and his wife Elizabeth Willing Powel, who was known for her influential role during the American Revolution. The Powel House is considered one of the finest examples of Georgian architecture in America, and is now a museum open to the public.

The house was designed by architect Samuel Rhoads, who was a prominent figure in the architectural scene of colonial Philadelphia. The exterior of the house features red brick with white trim, and is adorned with a simple but elegant doorway with a fanlight and sidelights. The interior of the house is equally impressive, with high ceilings, detailed woodwork, and ornate plasterwork. The rooms are spacious and filled with natural light, creating a sense of grandeur and elegance.

One of the most notable features of the Powel House is the ballroom, which is located on the second floor of the house. This room was used to host lavish parties and social events, and was known as the "most splendid apartment in the city".

The ballroom features a stunning plaster ceiling with intricate designs and a large crystal chandelier that illuminates the space. The room is also adorned with large mirrors, which were strategically placed to reflect the light and make the room appear even more spacious.

Over the years, the Powel House has undergone several renovations and restorations to preserve its historical and architectural significance. In the 1930s, the house was restored to its original condition by the Philadelphia Society for the Preservation of Landmarks, which had purchased the property. Since then, the house has been open to the public as a museum, providing visitors with a glimpse into the luxurious lifestyle of colonial Philadelphia's elite.

Today, the Powel House is a popular tourist destination, attracting visitors from around the world who are interested in American history and architecture. The museum offers guided tours of the house, allowing visitors to explore its various rooms and learn about its rich history. The house also hosts special events and educational programs, providing visitors with a unique and engaging experience.

In conclusion, the Powel House is a remarkable example of Georgian architecture and an important part of American history. Its elegant design and luxurious interior offer a glimpse into the lives of colonial Philadelphia's elite, while its historical significance serves as a reminder of the city's rich past. The house continues to be a beloved landmark in Philadelphia and a testament to the enduring legacy of America's colonial era.

Ghost sightings and unexplained phenomena

THE POWEL HOUSE, ALSO known as the Samuel Powel House, is a historic mansion located in Philadelphia, Pennsylvania. It was built in 1765 by Samuel Powel, a prominent political figure during the American Revolution who served as the last mayor of Philadelphia under British rule and the first mayor after the city's independence. Today, the Powel House is a popular tourist attraction and museum, open to visitors who want to learn about its history and architecture. However, the house is also known for its paranormal activity, with many reports of ghost sightings and strange occurrences throughout its long history.

One of the most famous ghost sightings in the Powel House is that of Samuel Powel himself. Visitors have reported seeing his apparition walking through the house or sitting in a chair in the parlour. He is often described as wearing his signature powdered wig and velvet suit, and seems to be going about his business as if he were still alive. Some visitors have also reported feeling a strange, eerie presence in the house, as if they are being watched or followed by an unseen entity.

Another ghost that is said to haunt the Powel House is that of a young girl. According to legend, the girl was the daughter of one of Powel's servants, and died in the house under mysterious circumstances. Her ghost is often seen wandering through the house, or playing in the garden outside. Some visitors have also reported hearing her laughter or the sound of her singing, even though there is no one around.

In addition to these two ghosts, there have also been reports of other paranormal activity in the Powel House. Visitors have reported hearing footsteps, doors opening and closing on their own, and strange knocking sounds coming from inside the walls. Some have even reported feeling a cold breeze or a sudden drop in temperature, even on warm days. Many of these strange occurrences seem to happen in the parlour, where Samuel Powel's ghost is most often seen.

Despite the many reports of ghost sightings and paranormal activity, the Powel House remains a popular destination for tourists and history buffs alike. Its beautiful architecture and rich history make it a fascinating place to visit, whether you believe in ghosts or not. And for those who do believe in the supernatural, the Powel House offers a unique opportunity to experience the eerie and unexplained firsthand.

The Powel House, also known as the Samuel Powel House, is an 18th-century mansion located in Philadelphia, Pennsylvania. Built in 1765 for Samuel Powel, who was the last mayor of Philadelphia under British rule and the first mayor after the American Revolution, the mansion has a long and storied history. Along with its rich history comes stories of unexplained phenomena that have occurred within the house.

One of the most commonly reported unexplained phenomena is the sound of footsteps. Visitors have reported hearing footsteps on the second floor of the mansion, even when there is no one else there. This is particularly strange because the second floor is not open to visitors, and there is no furniture or other objects that could cause the sound of footsteps.

Another commonly reported phenomenon is the appearance of apparitions. Several visitors have reported seeing a woman dressed in 18th-century clothing in various parts of the mansion. It is believed that this woman may be Elizabeth Willing Powel, Samuel Powel's wife. She was known for her intelligence and wit, and was a close friend of many of the Founding Fathers, including George Washington and Benjamin Franklin.

There have also been reports of doors opening and closing on their own, as well as objects moving without explanation. Some visitors have reported feeling a sense of unease or being watched while in certain parts of the house.

One particularly eerie experience was reported by a group of visitors who were touring the house after hours. They reported seeing a woman dressed in colonial clothing walking up the stairs. When they followed her, she disappeared into thin air. This experience has been reported by several other visitors as well.

Another strange occurrence that has been reported at the Powel House is the sound of music. Visitors have reported hearing music coming from various parts of the house, even when there is no one else there. Some believe that this music is coming from the spirit of Elizabeth Willing Powel, who was known to be a talented musician.

There is also a legend surrounding the Powel House that tells of a curse placed on the house by a slave. The story goes that Samuel Powel had a slave who was mistreated and eventually died in the house. Before the slave died, he placed a curse on the house, saying that it would never be happy. Some believe that this curse is responsible for the unexplained phenomena that have occurred in the house.

Overall, the Powel House has a rich history and a reputation for being one of the most haunted houses in Philadelphia. Visitors who are brave enough to explore the mansion after hours may experience some of the unexplained phenomena that have been reported over the years.

PHILLY'S PHANTOM ENCOUNTERS: EXPLORING THE CITY'S MOST HAUNTED PLACES

Chapter 8: The Academy of Music: Home to Ghostly Guests

The history and significance of the Academy of Music

The Academy of Music is a historical opera house located in Philadelphia, Pennsylvania. It was originally built in 1857 as a cultural centre and theatre for the city. The Academy of Music has played a significant role in the cultural and social life of Philadelphia for over a century, hosting world-renowned performers, debuts of famous operas, and many notable events.

The Academy of Music was designed by Napoleon LeBrun, who was a prominent architect during the 19th century. The exterior of the building is made of white marble, and it features a large entrance with a grand staircase leading up to the main hall. The interior of the building is ornately decorated, with gold leaf accents, chandeliers, and detailed frescoes covering the ceiling. The main hall seats over 2,900 people and has been praised for its acoustics, which are considered some of the best in the world.

The Academy of Music was built during a time when Philadelphia was one of the most prominent cities in the United States. The city was a centre of commerce and culture, and it was home to many wealthy families who were eager to support the arts. The Academy of Music was funded by a group of prominent citizens who wanted to create a space for opera and other cultural events.

The Academy of Music has played host to many famous performers over the years, including famous opera singers, musicians, and actors. One of the most notable performances at the Academy was the American premiere of Verdi's "Aida" in 1872. The Academy has also hosted performances by famous musicians such as Pavarotti, Sinatra, and The Rolling Stones.

In addition to its role as a performance venue, the Academy of Music has also been a venue for many important events in the city's history. It was the site of the first Republican National Convention in 1872, and it was used as a hospital during the Civil War. The building has also been the site of many important social events, including the Philadelphia Centennial Exhibition in 1876.

While the Academy of Music has played an important role in Philadelphia's cultural and social history, it has also had its share of challenges over the years. The building has undergone several renovations and restorations, and it has faced financial difficulties at times. Despite these challenges, however, the Academy of Music has remained an important part of Philadelphia's cultural life, and it continues to host performances and events to this day.

The Academy of Music is a historically significant opera house located in Philadelphia, Pennsylvania. Designed by Napoleon LeBrun and funded by a group of prominent citizens, the Academy of Music has played an important role in the city's cultural and social life for over a century. With its ornate interior, excellent acoustics, and long history of hosting famous performers and events, the Academy of Music is a true treasure of the city of Philadelphia.

Ghost sightings and unexplained phenomena

THE ACADEMY OF MUSIC, located in Philadelphia, Pennsylvania, is known not only for its rich history and architectural beauty but also for the reported paranormal activity that has occurred within its walls. This historic venue, built in 1857, is one of the oldest opera houses in the United States and has played host to countless notable performances and events over the years.

While the Academy of Music is primarily known for its cultural significance, many visitors and employees have reported paranormal occurrences within the building. One of the most commonly reported sightings is that of a ghostly figure dressed in white that has been seen on multiple occasions floating across the stage during performances. Some have speculated that this figure may be the spirit of a former actress or performer who met an untimely demise.

Another frequent occurrence is the sound of unexplained footsteps and other noises that seem to emanate from empty areas of the building. Many have reported feeling an eerie presence in the theatre, particularly in the balcony areas. Some visitors have reported feeling as though they are being watched or followed, even when they are alone.

Perhaps the most famous ghost story associated with the Academy of Music is that of the "Opera Ghost." This entity, said to haunt the building since the late 1800s, has been blamed for various unexplained occurrences throughout the years. Some believe that the ghost is the spirit of a former stagehand who fell to his death during the construction of the theatre, while others think it may be the ghost of a former performer who was disgruntled with her career.

Regardless of its origin, the Opera Ghost has become something of a legend at the Academy of Music. Many who have worked at the theatre over the years have reported strange occurrences that they attribute to the ghostly figure, including unexplained equipment malfunctions and other unexplainable phenomena. Some have even reported seeing the figure itself lurking in the shadows.

While these ghostly sightings and occurrences may seem frightening to some, many visitors and employees of the Academy of Music find them to be simply another fascinating aspect of the theatre's rich history. In fact, some have even reported feeling a sense of comfort or familiarity with the ghosts that they have encountered, as though they are simply part of the fabric of the building itself.

Whether one believes in ghosts or not, there is no denying the fact that the Academy of Music is a truly special place, with a history and culture that have left an indelible mark on the city of Philadelphia and the world of performing arts as a whole. And for those who are brave enough to venture into its hallowed halls, there may be more than just beautiful music to be found.

The Academy of Music in Philadelphia, Pennsylvania, has been a cultural landmark for more than 160 years. With such a long history, it's not surprising that many reports of unexplained phenomena have been associated with the venue. Over the years, visitors, staff, and performers have reported a variety of strange occurrences, from disembodied voices to ghostly apparitions.

One of the most famous stories involves a ghostly apparition known as "The Gray Lady." According to legend, the Gray Lady was a young opera singer who died suddenly while performing at the Academy of Music in the late 1800s. Her ghost is said to haunt the backstage area, and many people have reported seeing her ghostly figure walking through walls or standing in the wings.

Another ghostly tale involves a ghostly little girl. Some visitors have reported seeing a young girl dressed in old-fashioned clothing wandering the halls of the venue. It's unclear who this little girl might be, but some speculate that she might be the ghost of a child who died in the building.

Some people have also reported hearing unexplained sounds and voices in the Academy of Music. Some say they have heard strange footsteps or whispers, while others have heard phantom music playing. There have even been reports of people feeling a ghostly presence nearby, even when they are alone in a room.

One of the more unusual stories involves a ghostly presence known as "The Opera Dog." According to legend, this spectral canine appears backstage at the Academy of Music and wanders around, seemingly searching for something. Some speculate that the dog might have belonged to a performer or staff member who worked at the venue long ago, while others believe that the dog might be a residual energy imprint left behind by the many dogs who have accompanied performers to the venue over the years.

Another strange phenomenon that has been reported at the Academy of Music is the appearance of strange lights and orbs. Some people have reported seeing orbs of light floating through the air, while others have seen strange flashes of light or shadows moving across the walls. Some paranormal investigators believe that these anomalies could be caused by residual energy from the many performances that have taken place at the venue over the years.

Despite the many reports of unexplained phenomena, not everyone who has visited the Academy of Music has experienced anything out of the ordinary. Sceptics point out that many of the ghostly tales associated with the venue are just legends and rumours, with no basis in fact. However, for those who have had strange experiences at the Academy of Music, the unexplained phenomena remain a mystery.

Chapter 9: The Philadelphia Zoo: A Jungle of Ghosts?

The history and significance of the zoo

The Philadelphia Zoo is one of the oldest zoos in the United States, opening its doors to the public in 1874. Located in Fairmount Park, it covers an area of 42 acres and is home to more than 1,300 animals, representing over 42 species. The zoo has a rich history, and its founders had a unique vision for the establishment.

In the late 19th century, many people believed that zoos were primarily for entertainment purposes, and animal welfare was not a significant concern. However, the founders of the Philadelphia Zoo aimed to create a space where people could learn about and appreciate animals in their natural habitats. The zoo was designed to be a place of conservation and education, where visitors could observe exotic creatures up close and learn about their behaviours, diets, and habitats.

The Philadelphia Zoo has a significant place in American history. It was the first zoo to use a zoo train to transport visitors around the park, and it was also the first zoo in the country to breed animals in captivity successfully. During the Great Depression, the zoo suffered significant financial difficulties, but it continued to operate thanks to the tireless efforts of its staff and supporters. In the 1950s and 1960s, the zoo underwent a significant transformation, with the construction of new animal habitats and exhibits, including the World of Primates, Bird Valley, and the Big Cat Falls.

Today, the Philadelphia Zoo is home to a wide variety of animals, including lions, tigers, giraffes, elephants, and apes. It is also a leader in animal conservation efforts, with a focus on protecting endangered species and preserving habitats. The zoo has participated in numerous breeding and reintroduction programs, including the successful reintroduction of the Puerto Rican crested toad and the black-footed ferret.

Despite its reputation as a family-friendly attraction, the Philadelphia Zoo has its share of ghost stories and unexplained phenomena. Visitors and staff members have reported sightings of ghostly apparitions and strange noises throughout the park. Some of the most common ghost sightings are said to occur in the old Reptile House, which has been closed for many years.

One of the most famous ghost stories associated with the Philadelphia Zoo involves the former head zookeeper, Frank McDermond. McDermond passed away in the late 1960s, but some visitors and staff members claim to have seen him walking around the zoo after hours. According to some reports, he is always carrying a set of keys and appears to be checking the locks on the animal enclosures.

Another well-known ghost sighting involves a woman in a long dress, who has been seen wandering through the park at night. Some believe she may have been a former employee of the zoo, while others speculate that she may be the spirit of a woman who was killed in the area many years ago.

In addition to ghost sightings, the Philadelphia Zoo has been the site of other unexplained phenomena. Visitors have reported hearing strange noises, feeling cold spots, and experiencing feelings of being watched. Some have even reported seeing animals that should not be in the zoo, such as a lion that appeared out of nowhere and then vanished without a trace.

Despite these spooky tales, the Philadelphia Zoo remains a beloved attraction for visitors of all ages. Its commitment to animal conservation and education has made it a leader in the zoo industry, and its beautiful grounds and fascinating exhibits continue to draw visitors from all over the world. Whether you're a fan of animals or a lover of ghost stories, the Philadelphia Zoo is a must-visit destination in the City of Brotherly Love.

Ghost sightings and unexplained phenomena

THE PHILADELPHIA ZOO, located in the West Philadelphia neighbourhood, is one of the oldest and most beloved zoos in the United States. It opened in 1874, and over the years, it has become a popular destination for both locals and tourists. However, the zoo's history is not without its spooky and unexplained stories of ghost sightings.

One of the most well-known ghost sightings at the Philadelphia Zoo is that of a woman in white who is said to haunt the grounds. According to legend, the woman was a zookeeper who died on the job after being trampled by an elephant. Her ghost is said to appear near the elephant exhibit, and some visitors have even claimed to feel her presence when they visit the zoo.

Another ghostly tale associated with the zoo involves a lion named Brutus, who died at the zoo in the 1980s. Many visitors and zoo staff members have reported feeling a sense of unease or even a cold breeze when they walk by his former enclosure. Some have even reported hearing growling or roaring sounds coming from the exhibit when no lions are present.

There have also been reports of ghost sightings in the old Bird House at the zoo, which was built in the early 1900s and has since been renovated. Many visitors have claimed to see the ghost of a man in a brown suit wandering around the exhibits, even though there are no employees in the building.

In addition to these specific ghost stories, some visitors and employees at the zoo have reported more general feelings of unease or discomfort in certain areas of the grounds. For example, some have described feeling like they are being watched or followed, even though no one else is around. Others have reported feeling sudden drops in temperature or strange, unexplainable smells.

It's worth noting that while these stories are certainly intriguing, there is no concrete evidence to support any of them. It's possible that they are simply the result of overactive imaginations or a desire to add a bit of excitement to a visit to the zoo. Nevertheless, they add an interesting and mysterious element to the already-fascinating history of the Philadelphia Zoo.

As one of the oldest zoos in the United States, the Philadelphia Zoo is not just a popular attraction for animal lovers, but also a place where visitors have reported experiencing unexplained phenomena. From ghostly sightings to mysterious sounds, there have been several occurrences over the years that have left many visitors and employees spooked.

One of the most commonly reported sightings is that of a ghostly figure near the Big Cat Falls exhibit. According to witnesses, the apparition resembles a man in old-fashioned clothing, possibly from the early 20th century. Some have described him as having a stooped posture and walking with a limp. Others have reported seeing him vanish into thin air, leaving no trace behind.

Another area of the zoo that is said to be haunted is the World of Primates exhibit. Visitors and employees have reported hearing strange noises, including disembodied laughter and chattering, as well as feeling an eerie presence in the air. Some have even claimed to have seen the ghostly figure of a woman dressed in Victorian clothing.

One of the most famous ghost stories associated with the Philadelphia Zoo involves a lion tamer named Issac Van Amburgh. Van Amburgh was a renowned performer in the mid-19th century who gained fame for his daring stunts with big cats. However, he had a reputation for being cruel to his animals, and some believe that his ghost still haunts the zoo. Visitors have reported seeing a ghostly figure that resembles Van Amburgh near the big cat exhibits, and some have even claimed to have heard his voice.

In addition to these sightings, there have been reports of unexplained animal behaviour at the zoo. For example, several years ago, a group of gorillas suddenly became agitated and began throwing objects at their enclosure. Zookeepers were unable to explain the behaviour, and some have speculated that it may have been caused by paranormal activity.

There have also been reports of strange weather phenomena at the zoo. One visitor claimed to have seen a sudden and intense thunderstorm materialise out of nowhere, only to disappear just as quickly. Others have reported feeling sudden temperature drops or gusts of wind that seem to have no explanation.

While many of these occurrences remain unexplained, some believe that the Philadelphia Zoo's location may play a role. The zoo is situated on a historic estate known as The Solitude, which dates back to the late 18th century. It is possible that the land itself holds some kind of energy or residual spirits from the past.

Overall, the stories of ghost sightings and unexplained phenomena at the Philadelphia Zoo continue to intrigue and fascinate visitors. While some may be sceptical of these reports, many people have had their own unexplained experiences while visiting the zoo, leaving them wondering what other mysteries lie hidden within its grounds.

Chapter 10: The Betsy Ross House: A Revolutionary Spirit

The history and architecture of the Betsy Ross House

The Betsy Ross House is a historic house in Philadelphia, Pennsylvania. It is named after Betsy Ross, the woman who is said to have sewn the first American flag. The house is located in the heart of Philadelphia's Old City neighbourhood, just a few blocks from Independence Hall and the Liberty Bell. It is now a museum that attracts thousands of visitors each year, eager to learn about the life and work of this remarkable woman and the history of the American flag.

The Betsy Ross House was built in the early 1700s, making it one of the oldest surviving buildings in Philadelphia. It is a typical example of the architecture of the period, with a simple brick facade, a peaked roof, and a central chimney. The interior of the house is also typical of the time, with small rooms and low ceilings. However, the house has been extensively renovated over the years, and now features exhibits and displays that tell the story of Betsy Ross and her role in the creation of the American flag.

The house was originally built as a simple row house, but it was later expanded and renovated to accommodate Betsy Ross and her family. Betsy Ross lived in the house from 1776 to

1785, and during that time she was married twice and had five daughters. The house is now furnished with period pieces and exhibits that help to bring the story of Betsy Ross and her family to life.

In addition to its historic significance, the Betsy Ross House is also an important example of colonial-era architecture. The house is a fine example of the Georgian style of architecture, which was popular in the mid-18th century. The Georgian style is characterised by a symmetrical facade, a central entrance, and a peaked roof. The Betsy Ross House also features some elements of the Federal style of architecture, which was popular in the late 18th and early 19th centuries. The Federal style is characterised by a more ornate and decorative facade, with elements such as fanlights, sidelights, and pilasters.

Over the years, the Betsy Ross House has undergone many changes and renovations. In the late 19th century, it was restored to its original appearance, with the addition of a replica of the original porch. In the 1930s, the house was extensively renovated again, and new exhibits were added that highlighted the life and work of Betsy Ross. Today, the Betsy Ross House is a popular tourist attraction, and it remains an important part of Philadelphia's rich history and architectural heritage.

The Betsy Ross House is a remarkable example of colonial-era architecture and a testament to the life and work of one of America's most important historical figures. Its simple brick facade and peaked roof are emblematic of the Georgian style of architecture, while its exhibits and displays help to bring the story of Betsy Ross and her family to life. Whether you are a history buff or simply interested in Philadelphia's architectural heritage, the Betsy Ross House is a must-visit destination that is sure to leave a lasting impression.

Ghost sightings and unexplained phenomena

THE BETSY ROSS HOUSE, located in Philadelphia, Pennsylvania, is a historic house that was the home of Betsy Ross, the woman credited with sewing the first American flag. The house is a popular tourist attraction and museum, but it is also said to be haunted by the ghost of Betsy Ross herself. There have been numerous reports of ghost sightings and unexplained phenomena at the house over the years.

One of the most commonly reported ghost sightings at the Betsy Ross House is the apparition of Betsy Ross herself. Visitors have reported seeing a woman dressed in colonial clothing, often seen in the sewing room where Betsy Ross is said to have sewn the first American flag. Some have even reported feeling a chill or a presence in the room, even when it is empty.

Another reported ghost sighting at the Betsy Ross House is that of a young girl. Visitors have reported seeing a child's ghost running through the house or playing in the garden. It is believed that this may be the ghost of one of Betsy Ross's grandchildren, who died young.

There have also been reports of unexplained noises and voices at the Betsy Ross House. Visitors have reported hearing footsteps, doors opening and closing, and whispers. Some have even reported hearing the sound of a sewing machine, as if Betsy Ross herself is still at work in the sewing room.

In addition to ghost sightings, there have also been reports of other unexplained phenomena at the Betsy Ross House. Some visitors have reported feeling cold spots or sudden drops in temperature, even on warm days. Others have reported feeling a sense of being watched or followed, as if they are not alone in the house.

These ghost sightings and unexplained phenomena have led many to believe that the Betsy Ross House is indeed haunted. Some believe that the spirits of Betsy Ross and her family still reside in the house, while others believe that the house is a hotspot for paranormal activity due to its age and historical significance.

Regardless of the cause of these ghostly occurrences, they have only added to the intrigue and fascination surrounding the Betsy Ross House. The house remains a popular tourist destination, and visitors continue to report their own experiences with the supernatural. Whether or not the house is truly haunted, it is certainly a place of historical importance and cultural significance, and a fascinating piece of American history.

The Betsy Ross House, a landmark of Philadelphia, is not only famous for being the home of the woman who sewed the first

American flag, but also for its alleged hauntings. Visitors and staff have reported unexplained phenomena that they attribute to paranormal activity.

One of the most common ghost sightings in the Betsy Ross House is that of a woman in colonial attire believed to be Betsy Ross herself. She has been seen walking around the house, particularly in the upholstery shop where she is said to have worked on the American flag. Some visitors have also reported feeling a presence watching over them, as if someone is standing behind them, only to turn around and find no one there.

Another frequent sighting is that of a man dressed in a red coat, believed to be a British soldier from the Revolutionary War. It is said that he appears in the courtyard or outside the house, and some visitors have even reported feeling a chill in his presence.

The ghost of a little girl has also been seen in the Betsy Ross House, particularly in the basement. She is said to be about six years old, wearing a long dress and a bonnet. She has been seen playing with a ball or running around, giggling and laughing, only to disappear when someone approaches her.

Some people have also reported hearing unexplained noises, such as footsteps, doors opening and closing, or voices whispering. In some cases, objects have been reported to move on their own or disappear, only to reappear later in a different location. These phenomena are often attributed to the ghosts of past residents or workers who are still attached to the house.

One of the most famous paranormal experiences at the Betsy Ross House occurred in the 1940s when a group of electricians were working in the house. They reported hearing strange noises and feeling a presence watching over them. One of the workers even claimed to have seen the ghost of Betsy Ross herself, standing behind him and observing his work. The experience was so intense that the workers refused to continue working in the house and left the job unfinished.

Many of the reported ghost sightings and unexplained phenomena at the Betsy Ross House are believed to be connected to the history and significance of the house. As the birthplace of the American flag, it holds a special place in American history and may be a site of residual energy from past events. The house also served as a residence for multiple families over the years, and it is possible that some of these former residents still haunt the building.

Despite the many reported hauntings, the Betsy Ross House remains a popular tourist destination and a symbol of American history. Visitors are welcome to tour the house and even participate in interactive experiences, such as meeting "Betsy Ross" herself or trying their hand at colonial-era crafts. Whether visitors believe in ghosts or not, the Betsy Ross House offers a unique glimpse into the past and a chance to experience history firsthand.

PHILLY'S PHANTOM ENCOUNTERS: EXPLORING THE CITY'S MOST HAUNTED PLACES

Reflections on Philly's Phantom Encounters

Philadelphia is a city with a rich history dating back to colonial times, and as such, it is home to numerous historic and iconic buildings that are rumoured to be haunted. While each haunted location has its unique stories and legends, there are some common themes and similarities that can be observed.

One common theme is that many of the haunted places in Philadelphia are linked to famous historical figures, events, or tragedies. For example, the Eastern State Penitentiary is linked to notorious criminals such as Al Capone, and the Powel House is linked to the family of Samuel Powel, the first mayor of Philadelphia. Similarly, the Betsy Ross House is linked to the creation of the American flag and the birth of the United States.

Another similarity is that many of the haunted locations are large, imposing structures with a dark and foreboding atmosphere. The Eastern State Penitentiary, for instance, is a massive prison with imposing walls and a haunting Gothic architecture. The Philadelphia Zoo is also a sprawling location with large enclosures, creating a sense of isolation and unease in some areas.

Many of the haunted places in Philadelphia are also associated with violent or tragic events that occurred within their walls.

For instance, the Betsy Ross House is said to be haunted by the ghost of a young soldier who was killed on the premises during the Revolutionary War. The USS Olympia, a naval ship docked in Philadelphia, is said to be haunted by the ghosts of sailors who lost their lives in battle.

Another common theme among haunted places in Philadelphia is the presence of residual energy. Many of these locations have a long and storied history, with hundreds or even thousands of people passing through their doors. This energy is said to linger in the buildings and can be felt by those who are sensitive to it. The Powel House, for example, is said to be haunted by the ghost of a woman who died in childbirth and is said to be seen wandering the halls.

Finally, many of the haunted places in Philadelphia are popular tourist attractions, drawing visitors from all over the world. While the allure of these sites may be the historical significance or architectural beauty, the ghostly legends surrounding them only add to their appeal. Visitors to these locations often report feeling a sense of unease or even seeing apparitions, adding to the mystique and fascination of these places.

The haunted places in Philadelphia are varied in their histories and legends, but they share common themes and similarities. They are often associated with famous historical figures, events, or tragedies, and have a foreboding atmosphere. These locations also tend to have a residual energy that lingers from past events and are popular tourist destinations. Whether you believe in ghosts or not, the stories and legends surrounding these places are an integral part of Philadelphia's rich cultural heritage.

Exploring and investigating haunted locations can be a thrilling and eerie experience for those who are interested in the paranormal. It often involves visiting places that have a dark history or are known for their ghostly activity. Some people believe that these places are portals to another realm, while others think that the energy of past events and the people who lived or died there leave an imprint on the place, creating a haunting.

For those who embark on these explorations, it can be both exciting and nerve-wracking. They may feel a sense of trepidation and anticipation as they enter a place that is said to be haunted. The darkness, creaking floors, and shadows may all contribute to a sense of unease.

One common experience among those who explore haunted locations is the feeling of being watched. People report feeling as though they are not alone, even when there is no one else around. This feeling of being watched can be unsettling and contribute to a sense of fear or anxiety.

Another common experience is hearing unexplained noises or seeing objects move on their own. Doors may open and close, footsteps may be heard when no one is there, and objects may be moved or knocked over. These experiences can be particularly terrifying when there is no rational explanation for them.

People who explore haunted locations also report feeling physical sensations, such as cold spots, changes in temperature, or even being touched by unseen forces. Some people even report feeling a sense of pressure or heaviness on their chest, making it difficult to breathe.

Despite the potential for fear and anxiety, those who explore haunted locations often find it to be a fascinating and enlightening experience. They may learn about the history of a place, the people who lived there, and the events that took place. Some people also believe that they may be able to communicate with the spirits that are said to haunt the location, providing insight into the afterlife and the nature of death.

Exploring and investigating haunted locations can be a thrilling and eerie experience for those who are interested in the paranormal. While it can be a source of fear and anxiety, it can also be a fascinating and enlightening experience that provides insights into history, human nature, and the afterlife.

Ghost stories and folklore have been an important part of human culture for centuries. These stories serve many purposes, from explaining the unexplainable to providing entertainment and catharsis. They have evolved with time, but their significance has not diminished.

One of the most significant functions of ghost stories and folklore is to explain the unexplainable. Humans have always been curious about the world around them, and they have used stories to fill in the gaps of their understanding. Ghost stories, in particular, help to explain the mysteries of death and the afterlife. These stories provide comfort to those who are grieving and help them to come to terms with the idea of their own mortality.

Another important function of ghost stories is to provide entertainment. Humans have always loved a good scare, and ghost stories are a great way to get that adrenaline rush without putting oneself in any real danger. These stories are often told around a campfire or during a sleepover, and they have become a beloved pastime for many.

Ghost stories and folklore also play a significant role in cultural identity. They are often tied to a particular region or community and serve as a way to connect people to their heritage. For example, in Philadelphia, there are many ghost stories that are unique to the city and have become a part of its identity.

In addition to providing entertainment and cultural identity, ghost stories and folklore also have a therapeutic function. They can serve as a way for people to process their fears and anxieties. Hearing stories about ghosts and other supernatural entities can be a way for people to confront their own fears and overcome them.

Finally, ghost stories and folklore can also serve as a cautionary tale. These stories often have a moral lesson, teaching us to be careful of our actions and the consequences that come with them. They can help us to understand the importance of being mindful of the impact our actions have on others and the world around us.

Ghost stories and folklore have been an integral part of human culture for centuries. They serve many purposes, including explaining the unexplainable, providing entertainment, connecting people to their cultural identity, providing therapeutic benefits, and serving as a cautionary tale. Despite the many changes in society and technology, the significance of ghost stories and folklore remains, and they will continue to be an important part of our cultural heritage for generations to come.

Also by Edward Turner

Ghosts of Paris: Ten Haunted Places in the City of Love
Appalachian Nightmares: The Top 10 Creepy Creatures of the
Mountains
Asia's Top Ten Cryptids: Legends, Sightings, and Theories
Evil Women in History: Uncovering the Gruesome Crimes of
Ten Notorious Female Killers
Ghosts of London: Ten Haunted Places in The City
Ghosts of New York: Ten Haunted Places in The Big Apple
Missouri Nightmares: The Top 10 Chilling Legends
North America's Top Ten Cryptids: Legends, Sightings, and
Theories
Philly's Phantom Encounters: Exploring the City's Most
Haunted Places

About the Author

Edward Turner is a renowned author who specializes in exploring the realms of ghosts, the paranormal, and cryptids. With a captivating writing style and an insatiable curiosity for the unknown, Turner has garnered a dedicated following of readers who are captivated by his thrilling and eerie tales.

Born with an innate fascination for the supernatural, Turner has spent decades delving into the depths of paranormal phenomena, unearthing captivating stories and untangling mysteries that lie beyond the veil of the ordinary. His extensive research and meticulous attention to detail have earned him a reputation as a leading authority in the field.

Through his books, Turner expertly weaves together chilling accounts of encounters with ghosts, offering readers a glimpse into the ethereal world that coexists alongside our own. His ability to paint vivid portraits of spectral apparitions and convey the haunting atmosphere of haunted locations has made his works both spine-tingling and thought-provoking.

Turner's exploration of the paranormal doesn't stop at ghosts. He also dives into the fascinating world of cryptids—creatures that defy conventional explanation. His in-depth investigations into legendary creatures such as Bigfoot, the Loch Ness Monster, and the Chupacabra showcase his commitment to shedding light on these enigmatic beings.

With each page, Edward Turner's readers are drawn deeper into the enigmatic and unknown. His unique storytelling ability combined with his meticulous research has made him a sought-after author for those with an insatiable thirst for the supernatural. Whether delving into ghostly encounters or unraveling the mysteries of elusive cryptids, Turner's books offer a spine-chilling and immersive reading experience that leaves readers questioning the boundaries of our reality.

Edward Turner's works have earned critical acclaim and numerous accolades within the paranormal genre. He continues to explore the unexplained, captivating readers with his distinctive narrative style and unwavering dedication to unveiling the mysteries that lie hidden in the shadows.